WORLD WINDOWS

Senses

HEINLE
CENGAGE Learning

Y|S|G
A YBM COMPANY
Young & Son
Global, Inc.

How do you smell flowers?

Contents

senses

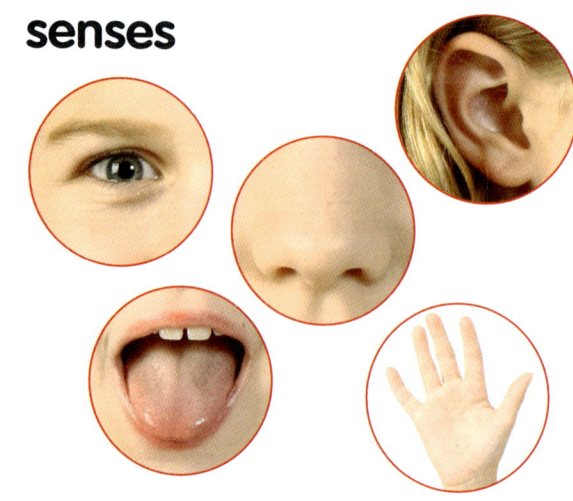

see

hear

smell

taste

touch

see

smell

hear

touch

taste

You have five senses.
You see, hear, smell, taste,
and touch.

How do you see?
You see with your eyes.

How do you hear?
You hear with your ears.

How do you smell?
You smell with your nose.

How do you taste?
You taste with your tongue.

How do you touch?
You touch with your hands.

You use different body parts for different senses.

Body Parts for the Five Senses

 eyes

 ears

 nose

 tongue

 hands

Which body part do you use for each sense?

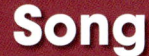

Song

Hear, Hear, I Can Hear

Hear, hear, I can hear
Everything around me.
I use my five senses.
Hear, hear, I can hear.

See, see, I can see
Everything around me.
I use my five senses.
See, see, I can see.

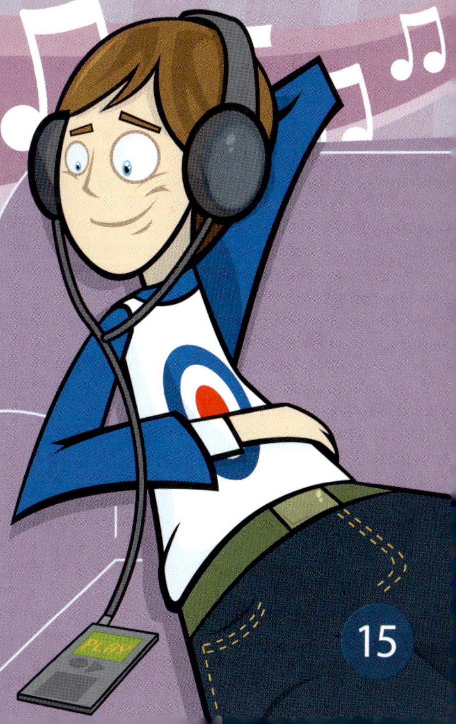

Index